Arise, Go Forth, Conquer!
(And other damn good advice...)

Rosie Hartmann

Go ahead, I dare you, adopt two of these!
Change. Your. Perspective.

Copyright

Copyright © 2019 Rosie M. Hartmann

Printed in the United States of America
Artwork created by Rosie Hartmann
First Printing, 2019

ISBN: 978-1-948326-05-6

www.studiorosie.com
Facebook: StudioRosie
rosie@studiorosie.com
eBay: rosiej

Dedication

To all of us mere humans who decide to take on a bigger battle. The battle against and for ourselves. For those who want more and for those who want to want more. This one is for all of us. We are all the underdog. So, let's all root for each one of us. ALL are welcome to join this unique club of those who are cheering for everyone including ourselves because damn it, we are worth it. And... a special shout out to all of you who have tossed my own advice in my face during my weak moments.

Acknowledgments

Two people rise above the rest at the onset of this book. My stepson Chris, for his harassment, joking with me in the darkest of times, and his foam-core-cutting-while-inhaling-glue skills. And Terry Stanley, for the no filter rule. (And her red pen skills for which, you, the reader should also be grateful, run on sentences can kill.)

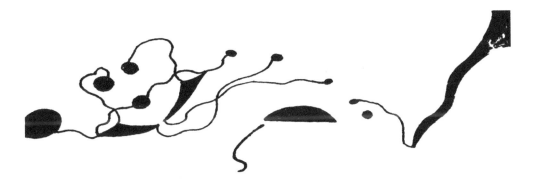

Introduction

This is the original artist's statement for the installation art this book was to be based upon. The installation did not happen so the book is going to carry the burden of the entire project (insert evil laughter here). Consider this introduction an appetizer. It will set the mood and maybe even surpass the rest of the book, as appetizers sometimes do.

The fact is we all must live by some set of "things". Those things are rarely simple. A complete list would require a far bigger mobile (or in this case book). Yet, within these "things" I live by are more things. Can you spot them all?

This entire thing started out as a thing. One seemingly small goal: Do an installation. So here is to getting a thing within a thing done. Multitasking! Always! (That is yet another of those "things" I live by) And just to prove I am living by those things:

I collaborated on two pieces with my incredible niece, Hannah. (This is also a thing within a thing, I did collaborate which is in the mobile, I also passed art on; that is not in the mobile or in this case book)

I am going to make a book out of all the things in this set of things. How does that work its way in to the things you ask? Making books is the most fun rabbit hole of all. I shall willingly jump down into that rabbit hole and pray the entire way I do not end up with Vol 10 of the Damn Good Advice Series. (Shameless self-promotion: Book should be available May 1st on Amazon, which will be pushing myself as I have not started it yet) (Update: at the time of this typing it was still unfinished but with a new release date of April 19th.)

Fears sure I will hug them and love them, by publicly saying I will do a failure is imminent installation. 1st installation; I was clueless oh so clueless, and probably still am. (And, as you know, the installation art did flop, right on its belly from a 10-foot-high diving platform.

Worse yet I told everyone I would put 'em ALL on eBay at $5 after the show. Now everyone can watch as they succeed to new heights or go down in a ball of flames either of which I will handle gracefully as that will be the end of the installation. (More shameless self-promotion: eBay sale date starts May 1st because I am a moron Dancing Tall on May 1st) (Well, that plan went to hell. Hopefully you are reading this book before the eBay sale since I changed the time line to go with the flow)

I did show some damn discipline in this endeavor as well. You see I have 500 Peeps sitting on my table. Not only did I not eat them, I also did not stop the process of this installation to make a Peep Sculpture to enter the RAM Peep show. I desperately wanted to. (Eat them I mean … I still want to eat them) (Update: I no longer want to eat the colorful hockey pucks)

Laced throughout all these things I hope you will find some humor because God knows I tried to lace the humor throughout it all. And of course, that is another thing within this set of things I live by. So, carry on and do enjoy and laugh a little at me or with me. Either way is just fine because (yup, another thing) laughter is the soul's reward.

Arise Go Forth Conquer

Arise from the depths of your own personal hell. We all have a reality that is our own personal Hell. Go forth straight towards the next fan blowing unsavory things your way. Conquer all that is tossed at you up to and including rat infestations, a room full of mosquitos, and the everlasting unrelenting heat of places like Vietnam.

It does not matter what your version of Hell is. We all come from a place that scarred us somehow. The universe keeps putting us into perilous places one after another. The powers-that-be will continue to do this to us until time ends. There is no end to the rotten salads being tossed in our direction. And thank all-that-is-good for that. That one fact ensures that unicorns are real, miracles happen, and rainbows are beautiful. You have the power (and contained within this book some powerful tools that will screw you up as much as they will help.... because Balance.)

Go forth into the world and take it all on. Make the commitment to embrace what good the world showers on you right after washing off all it vomited on you.

And then.... Conquer it. Of course, once you do this, be aware this is a rinse and repeat scenario. Full disclosure Arise, Go Forth, Conquer is a circular argument. Further reading on that topic forthcoming.

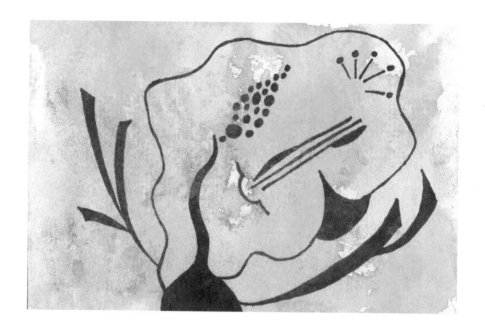

Pet Fear, Embrace Fear, Name Fear, Face Fear, Love Fear

The idea of No Fear enrages me. I love fear. I crave fear. I need fear. You can too. You should. (I assure you I am not a thrill-seeking nut job or complete whacko).

Here is how. Commit to thinking about the fear (petting the fear) and consider doing something about the fear (embracing the fear). These two steps could take a day or a week...there is no time limit the point is not to scare yourself into doing nothing. Take your sweet time.

Next, list your fears out. All of them even the ones that make you feel like bugs are crawling over your skin, especially the ones that you find almost impossible to write down. ALL of them, every single one (Naming the Fear).

Rank them least scary to most scary. There is not right or wrong here I could care less if your biggest fear is a spider and your least scary thing is airplane rides or success. This is you. You are special in your ranking, no one else will rank their fears like you do because you one of a kind.

Next...confront and conquer the easiest one. Face the Fear. Then repeat. One a year or one a week, you are a success. Let me tell you some I have faced: bridges over water, stairs with openings, sensory deprivation, self-sabotage, success, and the ever-awful snakes.

Once you have emerged victorious from your first couple of battles you will have built up some confidence, developed amazing skills at increasing that confidence and you've learned to love overcoming the obstacles. This is loving the fear. It starts with just facing the easiest fear.

If your they impatient type, you might decide to expediate the process and climb a flight of open stairs and crawl into the sensory deprivation chamber full of snakes. My advice? Go for it BUT only after building the confidence to scare yourself even more. This process is addicting. Show a bit of caution but adjust your pace when you are comfortable with it.

The Greatest Love of All Is the Love That Comes From Within

I am not an advocate of "you can't love anyone unless you love yourself". I loved and lost many times over before I loved myself.

I am, however, a fan of loving all the aspects of who I am. Even the screwed-up parts of me. I even name them. For example, one who lives inside me is Little Monster. He is very angry. He was the self-sabotager of my life. I had a chat with him. He was like a child with no boundaries, no rules and never allowed to wreak havoc within the guidelines. (And yes, this does feel like a bit of my masculine side. Don't shrink back! We all have both male, female, and primal sides)

I set the rules and now when I need a little more oomph to a situation, I call on Little Monster. Or if I need some fun, I call on Inner Child. Every time I identify and chat with an aspect of myself, I grow, gain clarity and love myself more.

Little Monster, Swimmer, Inner Child, Inner Sadness, Inner Calm, Primal Me, Future Me, Past Me, Present Me.... and even the worst of them all Inner Turmoil and I have chatted. We work together. I am sure there is a psychologist or ten that would label these voices in my head as bad. But let me ask you this; If they all lead me to the greatest love of all how bad can they be? Bring the inner voices on, because listening to them IS the greatest expression of the greatest love of all.

Fake It Till You Make It Is A Legit Tactic

I am pretty convinced I fake everything. Please, no sloppy innuendoes here, even they might be warranted.

You do not have to be good at anything when you first start. Just fake it. Own the fact that you have not made it and suddenly people will think you are so smart and have clearly made it.

It makes no sense. None. Yet, it is a fact. Combine that fact with the desire to make it and you will make it. Learn and grow and become better. Suddenly faking it got you there.

We must earn the confidence of making it, but we need a certain type of confidence to get there. It is yet another of life's catch 22's. So just own it and fake it while getting through the stuff that gets you to the land of "Truly Confident".

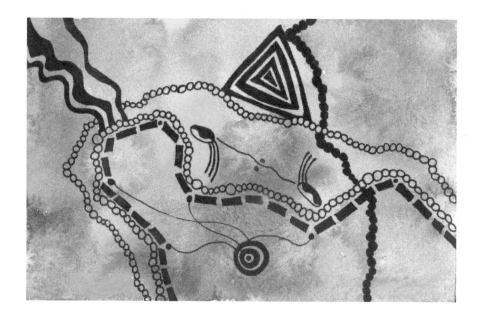

Be Bold in Everything You Do

Mediocrity sucks. Boldness stands out. Risk gets rewards. Confidence is sexy. Wear boldness like your favorite pair of broken in boots or the jeans that fit like no other pair of jeans. (And if you are male.... a car that needs oil changes like no other? Sorry the frame of reference is off on this one for me BUT I am being bold and owning it!)

Boldness means wearing the inner you on the outside. State the opinions you have. Wear the clothes you want to. Don't wear the makeup you don't want to. Own a Chevy if you want to (honestly, that was painful to write...I'm Ford all the way. Please feel free to send hate mail). So what if I or anyone else wants to judge you? That is their personality flaw and is never allowed to affect your boldness. Ever.

To be honest my frame of reference issue is probably because my Ford DID need oil changes like no other. (It was a Mustang, what can I say?)

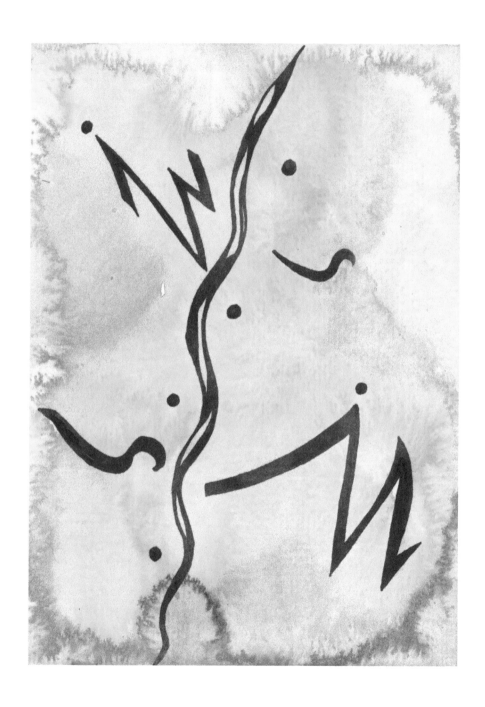

Nature Is the Soul's Workout

Who cares about all the studies saying nature helps you in so many ways? I do not. The minute you go out into nature for the pure sake of what it can do for you, you have lost.

Go out into nature because your soul needs it. Go out into nature to feel the wind sweep around you (especially when it is a powerful wind...EXHILIRATION). Listen to the waves crashing. Watch the birds chasing each other. Avoid the geese though unless it is to watch them flying in the perfect harmony V shape in the sky somewhere not directly above you.

Look at the night skies with awe and the clarity of how insignificant we are. Insignificance is beautiful. In the bigger picture it allows you to take life less seriously.

Look at the natural patterns. Most importantly, be reminded that we are animals of nature too. You can learn so much about yourself by understanding you have qualities of nature. Me, I am like the wind. Calm or powerful and the result of things beyond my control yet influencing the path I follow. How about you?

Avoid the Rabbit Hole

Have you ever dusted the ceiling fan? I rest my case. This type of rabbit hole is very dangerous. You should not proceed with caution. You should not talk yourself out of the danger. You should not slowly back away. You should run to the hills, run for your life.

The rabbit hole cannot be underestimated, ever. Rabbit holes can pop up at any time on any topic. You must be vigilant and never hunt for rabbit holes. Your success on this topic is dependent on your brain. Be nice to your brain as it is the first line of defense against rabbit holes. Your brain is the one counseling you...Do not look up at the ceiling fan unless it is running. Your brain is the one saying to you dusting does not include the ceiling fan.

Pay attention now. This is the most important thing "ceiling fan" can be substituted for just about anything. This is because just about anything can be a rabbit hole. The list of things is endless. You must be vigilant.

I hope most of you understand why you must be vigilant. In case you do not comprehend the dangers let me lay them out for you. Rabbit holes suck your time dry. They leave no room for anything but delusions. You will try very hard - at every turn of the rabbit hole - to convince yourself it will only take a few more minutes. It turns out to be years. Meanwhile all your goals and aspirations are put on hold. For what I ask you? For the "ceiling fan"?

Quit Fighting Yourself

I can't take it. I see you in the left corner and I see you in the right corner of the ring. You look prepared to battle yourself to the death. Being a betting gal, I am putting my money on the referee. I am pretty sure that of the four of us, I am the only winner. The referee can't win, that would be illegal. You will lose one way or the other.

You are fighting yourself for some reason. Probably you are not listening to your gut instinct, which is telling your right now what makes things all better. Or maybe it is fear. Or maybe you enjoy beating yourself up. I have news for you, I won the bet AND you can fix all the issues that are causing you to fight yourself. A great start anytime you find yourself about to take the gloves off and have at it with yourself is to remember: Listen to your gut, face your fear and/or be nice to yourself.

Hopefully you do not let me win any more bets. I could become addicted to the winning.... (sneak peek into Vol 2)

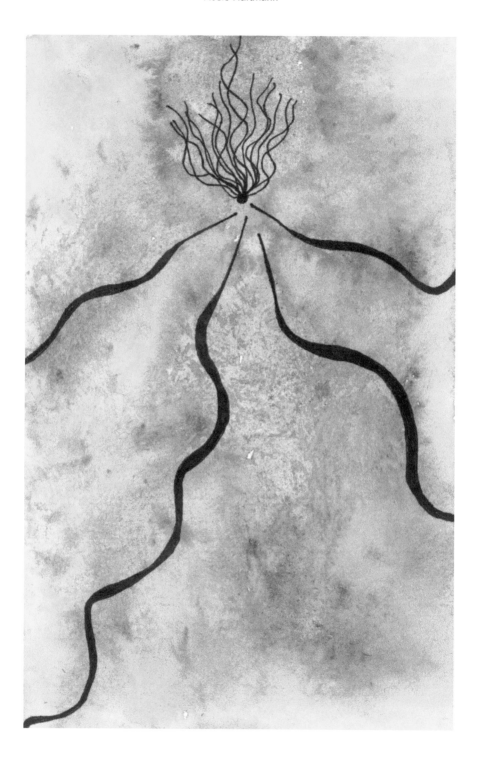

You Are Tall Dance Tall

We've all heard the generalizations: You are short you won't go far. Blondes have more fun (there for no one else does). You are female you will get screwed over because of that. You are male so you don't have emotions. Your tattoos will hold you back. And my personal favorite if you do not embrace God you will not go far.

Blasphemy! You are tall, you have fun, there are tons of ways to not get screwed over. The 14 tattoos I have never held me back. I have seen grown men cry. I prefer spiritual to dogma.

What happened to positive encouragement? Dance to your tune and all the positives it offers you because the negatives (everything that says you are somehow less) are straight up bullshit. You have the power to make those negatives meaningless. You also have the power to never ever ever ever spread another thing like that. And if you do, I say the negatives still have power over you. Why would you be okay with that?

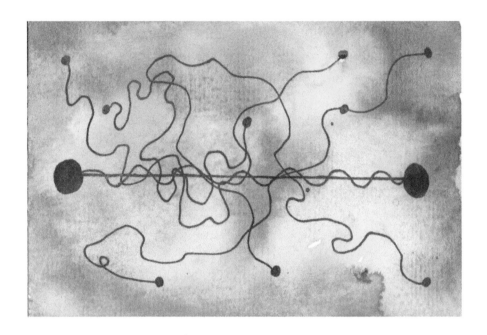

You Do Need A Recombobulation Area

For those of you that do not know what I mean by a recombobulation area let's look at Milwaukee's General Mitchell International Airport.

You go to the airport to take a trip to Montego Bay or-you-know-Detroit. You go through taking off your shoes, emptying your pockets, opening your laptop, getting scanned, needing a pat down and finally collecting all your things from the trays. This all happens in about three minutes. You are discombobulated. The very next thing you see in the Milwaukee airport is the Recombobulation Area. Heaven! It's a space to put yourself back together again.

That was just three minutes. You get a space with a few chairs and a bit more room then the end of the line at the check point. Now imagine an entire day of being taken apart. See? You do need a recombobulation. Go make yourself one, right now!

Always Be Working on A List of Ten

How do you ensure that you are creating the life you want to have? The answer is The List Of Ten. The List of Ten is a group of things you have as goals. Attainable goals that are broken up into a highly strategic group of actions.

5 personal things that help you to love you. Growing your hair out, spending more time in nature, losing 10 or 100 lbs., refining your style or working on the qualities you do not like (come on - we all have some unattractive qualities...Even me! I had fierce anger issues) Or the most empowering: facing fears. Yes, I am asking you to work on YOU,

2 career/hobby goals help you to feel satisfied and accomplished. Maybe it is learning new skills or getting more into a hobby that could become more than a hobby. Maybe it is winning $2000 in a Texas hold 'em tournament. Hey It could happen! It did for me 6 books and 1 year after I started playing Texas Hold 'Em I won $2000. All these things add to the feeling of confidence and value you place on yourself.

3 Life goals that you can track over time. A jar of change for a dream trip, a house buying savings account or one for retirement, a snazzy car or owning an alpaca. I mean for real? Why do all the hard work if there are no big rewards?

Now four times a year check in on these things. Over time if nothing is happening with them maybe you need to examine if they are the right things and change 'em up. As they get done, replace them with new things.

This List Of Ten will give you direction and help you be an object that stays in motion. I mean who wants to move with no direction?... I simply can't go back and forth like those whack-a-balls that never stop moving. (Scientific Name: Newton's Cradle. I hope we both learned something new today)

Take the Risk Especially the Educated Risk

Would you jump out of a plane? Would you jump out of the same plane with a parachute? How about a tandem parachute jump? This all sounds terrifying to me (something that is still on my list of fears to face). One of these options is the educated risk. I understand that if I am jumping out of a plane with another person in control it is safer for me. That (hopefully extremely good-looking guy or gal whichever you prefer) is going to pull the cord. I will not be at risk of freezing up, hyperventilating and missing the moment to save my life as I hurtle toward the ground. Good looking guy, life saved, fear faced; it seems like a good call to me that the educated risk is the correct one here.

All risks are just like this, without the life ending moment in most cases. You can explore the ideas of all risks to make an educated decision, a thoughtful decision, a better decision. Risk demands some guts. The amount of guts it takes is directly dependent up on the brain cells you use in deciding how to take the glorious fall out of a plane.

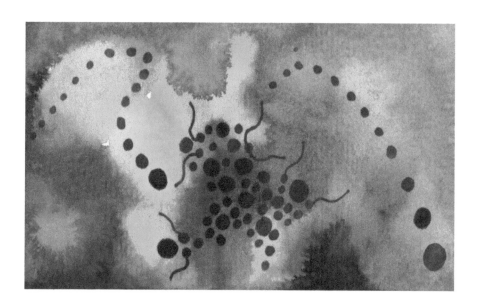

Dance Even in The Darkness

Did you know half of your time on earth (depending upon geographic region, daylight savings time and other manmade or natural occurrences) is spent in the darkness???

I am unwilling to give up half of my time (or so) for dancing due to being in the dark.

Dancing is always good. Dance in the streets. Dance in the Darkness of all the world tosses at you, better yet dance naked in your home, just keep dancing and then dance more.

Sure, times might get rough and tough like a fan with excrement blowing at you right after you got hit by a flock of birds in the middle of losing the championship game. Dancing helps you navigate through all of it. If nothing else have someone shoot some video and post it. Dancing in the darkness and laughing in the darkness is telling yourself it will be okay. Granted sometimes it is not okay, but that is okay and does happen too. Dancing will ensure even in rough times there is still goodness to be had.

Failure Is Nothing but Target Practice

Failure is your friend. It has much to teach you young one. And me too for that matter.....

This book started out as an installation for an art exhibition. The installation went down in a blaze of glory, the flames spontaneous and brilliant. I shall tell no lies - I did shed a tear over it. Then I asked my perturbed self; what could have been done differently or better?

Holy smokes, the list was long and dumb. Then I made a game out of it. What if I did it all differently? My brain exploded! Truth be told it probably broke in the process. Now that I had been through the ENTIRE process right up to the installation part (the one with the brilliant flames) I understood exactly what I would do differently.

Right then. Right there. I knew the only way to truly honor the Big Fail was to complete the plan. Afterwards, I'd pick myself back up and go for Attempt Deux, the attempt that will be better, bolder and possibly warrant even more brilliant flames.

Attempt Deux will not have a single piece of art that includes a rule/guideline about failing. I jinxed myself! My God what was I thinking? It is clear to me in some ways the message of my art is self-fulfilling prophecies. (I did warn you the list of things to do differently included dumb things)

Let me add some shameless self-promotion....Follow along for details on the next art installation adventure. And if you need therapy for your own target practice, drop me an email rosie@studiorosie.com. We are in this together. So, if you want to laugh about how you learned the things you did, I shall laugh with you, at you or in whatever direction you need me to.

A Circular Argument Is Always A Circular Argument No Matter the Disguise

"You spin me right 'round baby like a record baby." In circles you will go. Oh, the merry-go-round of all situations. This is a tactic of those who want to win, they wear you down running in all those circles. You will find yourself out of breath, ideas and comebacks. Still, you carry on, oblivious to the fact that a circle always follows a circular path.

Once identified, you regain the power. Notice, I did not say you win. No person can win a circular argument. The trick is to recognize it. The signs are simple. Each leg of this journey leads back to a singular place. You can try a different approach on the next leg and you still end up in the same place.

Why oh why do these arguments happen? I am going to tell you. Dominance...One party or the other is trying to assert dominance over the other with a win. It is a dirty, sneaky and often fun tactic.

The minute you believe (to the very bits of your soul) that the win is not necessary, you win! You can't believe in this idea for the sake of the win though. See, that is the pitfall...My answer IS a type of circular argument until you truly believe it is not.

Show Some Damn Discipline

All this advice is only good if you show the discipline to follow it. All the good intentions of not eating the entire bag of M & Ms is only as good as the discipline behind it. You see where I am going right? ... All your dreams, desires, wants and things come down to "show some damn discipline." (SSDD)

To be more specific, hold yourself to the 80% Rule. You didn't really think I was going to demand 100% of any of us puny mortals who are prone to human nature did you? Make sure you enjoy that 20% of the time enough to carry you through the other 80%, because that 80% gets hard by the time you hit 50% or so. Horrid stuff getting close to 80%, but rather then tell you that you can do it, I will just holler at you show some damn discipline.

My intention is not to be mean. I don't want to tell you that you can do it in reference one thing. I would rather show you a way you can do it on everything. Discipline for the win.

Get A Damn Hobby Even If You Suck at It

Are you hanging in there with me? Do you see the unwritten rule? All rules get tangled up in each other for the good and the bad.

That is how hobbies work. One leads to another or gets tangled into another. Each one helps or hurts another. Contradictions abound in life. Hobbies can help you to figure that out.

Hobbies lead to absurd laughter. The spaghetti incident of knitting is still one I laugh at today. The manipulation of yarn taught me about eye/hand coordination, and my lack of it. If you let those pastimes teach you, epiphanies abound. Revelations happen, laughter will be had. Magically, effortlessly, you have improved and added to yourself without even trying. Let the adventures commence.

Screw the Distractions Keep Your Eye On the Prize

We are going to get all Beastie Boys on this one. Sabotage! (Really, my favorite song by them and being able to reference it...HUGE)

Oops, tangent. Sorry.

My favorite form of sabotage is that of the self kind. It is the easiest to avoid and the quickest to carry out. If I had a dime for every time I shot myself in the foot I could have a kitchen floor tiled with dimes. (It would take 90,000 in case you were curious. Truth. 90,000) I may have exaggerated about the number of times I shot myself in the foot.

The prize is the goal you are trying to attain. The distractions are the self-sabotage. Now why do we go and do that? Next time you notice this happening, put a dime in the jar. Hopefully you never have enough to tile your kitchen floor. Maybe the dimes made you aware of these times. However, a nice dinner out; well at least you got something outta those self-sabotage moments.

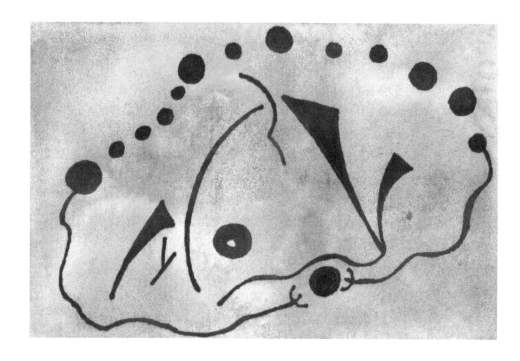

Release the Endorphins Stretch

Stand up right now and if someone is with you, they should video this moment. Feet shoulder width apart. Arms up in the air stretched out. Make yourself look like an X. Hold for 30 seconds and try not to smile. Don't like that position? Shesh! Fine then hop into the Wonder Woman pose. Legs shoulder width apart hands in a fist at each hip with your elbows sticking out. 30 seconds. Try not smile (or hit anyone with your elbows for that matter). Post the video online, especially if you broke into goofy laughter.

This is the "assume the position" of success and super heroes. It releases happy, healthy, fun, endorphins. Endorphins are your friend; they provide the chemical confidence boost we all need here and there and it's 100% natural.

You are biologically built to fake it till you make it with this endorphin thing. Studies have shown that this position done right before a stressful event leads to a more successful outcome. In interviews, those who have done this prior to the interview have been said to appear happier, less intimidated and more confident.

Who knew? Not only do I think you can fake it till you make it so does your body.

The Distance Between A Mistake and A Happy Accident Is Almost Nonexistent

Look at all the wonderful things about the time and space you are at right now. Then add up the number of mistakes it took you to get right here right now. It is astonishing how much you must screw up in life!

If you think we are not all nincompoops tripping our way through life, you are incorrect. From the moment we try to stand we did not understand that falling is next, nor did we know that walking is the best. (although I am an advocate of the army crawl...it is stealthier)

Every time I screw up on a piece of art, I do not call it a mistake I look for the happy accident (thank you Bob Ross). Sure, I look for what I may have learned too. I find more joy and adventure in finding what is good about the mistake.

I am not talking about the proverbial silver lining that is entirely another topic. I am talking about the unexpected piece of brilliance that this mistake will lead to. It is like a butterfly flapping its wings in India.

Sure, a butterfly can flap its wings in India, but a toad can also fart in the Amazon. So, every mistake might be a toad farting in the Amazon and who knows what change those winds will make?

Look Around You Right Now, Repeat Daily

Being "in the moment" is very vague. I sort of hate the statement. What the hell does it mean to be in the moment anyway? I am alive and I am here, thus I am in the moment.

Instead be aware! See the moment. Name the things you see. This practice will show you how much you can see; colors, weather, moods, danger, opportunities, textures and more. The list of things we see is endless.

Do it daily, or more. Things change daily, hourly and by the minute. Hell, they even change in a second. If you make the practice of look around you right now even just once a day you will suddenly be all in the moment. This practice opens the unseen world of awareness.

Let me caution you though it is like taking the sunglasses off on a bright day. At first you want to shrink back. After a period of adjustment, you bask in the conditions of the light.

Discover What Is Missing in Your Candy Bowl

Life is meant to be enjoyed. What is that one tiny little thing you can add to your candy bowl to provide daily enjoyment? If you can answer that, never let that one little thing go. It is my daily Starbucks coffee for me. That one "little" is so much more. My gals at my Starbucks are the BEST! Not only do I get coffee, I also get kindness, laughter and a beautiful start to each day. Some days that coffee and those gals are the one bright spot. Truth be told, they are half the reason I made it through some tough times. It does not matter what happens, $3 a day goes to Starbucks. During my divorce I gave up lots of things to ensure that one thing remained mine.

If you do not have an answer find one. Is it a routine to start your day that puts the day on your terms? Is it sometime in nature? Is it a special chocolate you have once a day? Is it 30 minutes that is just for you? There are so many little things for you to choose from. So, go out and choose now. No matter who you are this is something you can do for you. Just one small little thing. It is you telling yourself daily... "Self you are special!"

By the way, the Starbucks guys are pretty awesome too. I would hate to leave them out because they are a part of what is in my candy bowl too.

5 Things A Day Keeps the Housework Away

Quit letting things pile up. You just defeat yourself when you do. The minute you get overwhelmed you shut down a little don't you? The beauty of the rule I am about to explain in detail is self-serving, adaptable to more than just house work and your future self will thank you. (shameless foreshadowing of Vol 2)

Here is how it goes. I walk into the house at the end of my work day. I fill the dishwasher and that counts as one of the five. While the dishwasher is running, I take the garbage out, which also counts as one. When I come in from taking out the garbage, I put a new bag in the garbage and that too, counts. I can't help that I loathe garbage and therefor it gets more of a count. (See I told you... self-serving). My next step is to look at the pile of mail that builds up of the course of days, the mostly junk mail unless I missed something pile. I toss the junk in the recycle bin, also counting as one.

Now it gets complicated. The dishwasher is not done running and emptying it would count as one, but I am already at four. I want to be done. The decision is made, the dishwasher gets emptied tomorrow. My last step is to sweep quickly.

All you really need to do is assign the point value to any task. Dish washing is always two for me. Garbage is always two. Sweeping is one. Cleaning a counter is one, cleaning all the counters is five. You see what I am doing here?

You have 7 days in a week. You get one day off a week. That is 30 things every week. You will never again, outside of seasonal deep cleaning if that is the type of person you are (bravo), spend entire days cleaning. The beauty of it is you get to pick your day off. Everyone should have a mental health break from the five. Choose your day wisely or Future Self-will yell at you. (That is to be avoided at all costs, Future Self is sometimes mean and harsh)

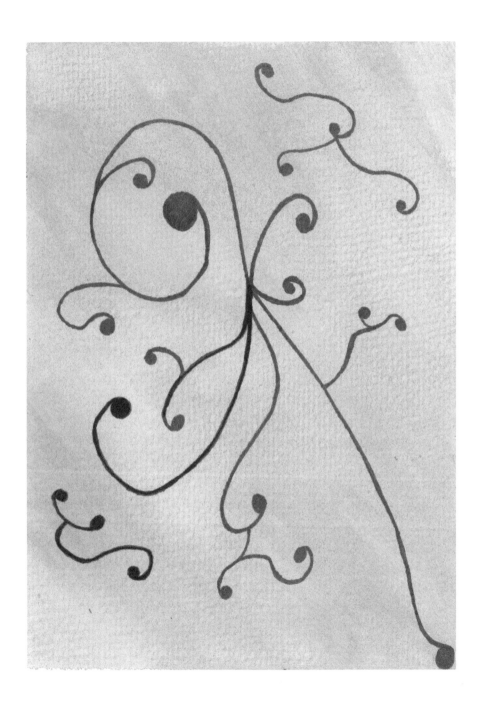

Rabbit Holes Are Much Fun

You have been there. The rabbit hole of Gloriousness, the rarest of all rabbit holes. The one that is WORTH IT. Unlike the "ceiling fan"- you will recall - which is not. This rare breed of rabbit hole appears less than one out of one hundred rabbit holes. Many times, it is overlooked. Leading to a successful rare rabbit hole being comparable to winning the lottery. How do you identify this type of rabbit hole?

It ties into one or more other rules. For example, is this a rabbit hole that aids and abets your List of Ten? Is this a rabbit hole that could count as an entire five things done? Perhaps it is a hobby you might suck at. If you can make the argument that you have accurately identified this rare happening, run straight into it, head first if you like. Explore, enjoy and let the adventure begin.

If not.... run to the hills, run for your life!

Contain Your Chaos

Let's talk about a bucket of water. How much dirt can be put into the water before it is unusable?

What if your sphere of influence is the bucket of water? What are you adding to that bucket of water? At what point have you made the water unusable for anyone?

Your chaos, your bad mood, your drama (for the love of all that is good, your DRAMA). This is all dirt. You have a choice, toss it into the bucket or ensure that your chaos does not affect the water. It is still your stuff and you are entitled to it just because you are a descendant of Neanderthals. HOW you handle your chaos and the bucket is up to you.

Now consider all the buckets that are close to each other. Rarely are we alone. It is possible to help others clear the water in their buckets too. It is all dependent on HOW you handle your own chaos.

Now that I have condensed this down to a water problem and a global solution, is it clearer? No? Just think about a time and a place you have been where one person ruined an entire work day, event or whatever. Their water was muddy and turbulent enough to affect yours.

Don't be that person whose bucket is dirty and splashing. Nobody wants to clean up the mess, especially not you.

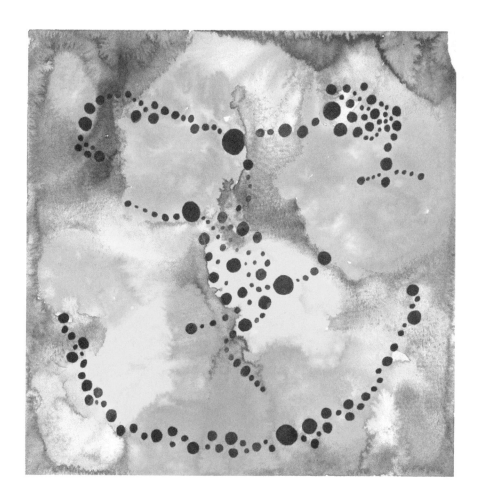

Who Cares If You Fit In

Where are you right now? If it is not in the comfort of your own recombobulation (no, I am not sure that is a word that counts in scrabble, it does counts at my airport and in my world) space do you feel like you fit in? Be honest - you do not have to say it out loud, this is a rhetorical question. One of those questions you are answering just for yourself, not for me.

You don't have to answer for my sake. I already know we all feel like we don't fit in more often then we feel like we do. Get over it. Who cares? There is a deeper truth to be had.

We are all different. Yet we all fit in the world. I know that because we are here. You feel. You get sick, you dream, and you fear. These things make you fit in. They make us all fit in. Rejoice in where you are because currently, in this place, it is where you belong simply because you are there.

Feeling like you don't fit in and not liking where you are at; now that is two separate things. One you can change. That is the challenge in this advice. Do you feel like you do not fit in or do you just hate where you are at?

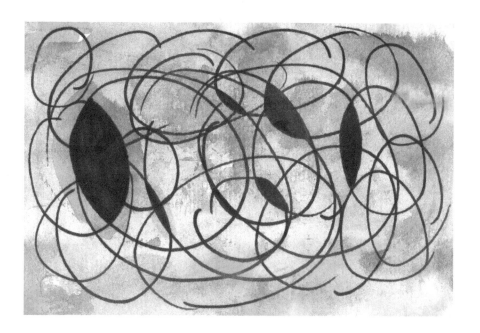

Collaborate More

Ok, opportunity knocks. What do you do? (I would like to add a long dramatic pause here, but it is a book, so please imagine it) Ok, but what do you really do?

I have talked to many photographers in the last year. Given them my number and said, "I can help you if you are looking to make a career of it." What did I hear back? Crickets. Mostly.

The benefits of collaboration are ridiculous. Half the work for double the return. If - it is done right. First you must recognize a good opportunity. Second you have to say yes. Third you must bring your best self to the game.

Possible side effects do include disappointment and hard work. Possible benefits new ideas, good mojo and meeting new people. Growth is not done alone. At some point you are not enough to continue your own growth in anything. Even if you end up disappointed in the results, you will grow.

This piece was drawn by me and painted by my niece, Hannah. What a wonderful thing! She embraced the opportunity to be a part of something bigger then both of us. As for me, I know what I got out of it...Multi-Tasking (Yup, another one in Vol 2), time with my niece, half the work and the extra benefit of seeing her mix colors in a way I would never do but like and might have to consider now.

Rules: Learn, Perfect, Repeat

Yup, another rule that is guaranteed to make you look and feel like an ass. If I were being reality based, the title would be "Rules, Learn, Look Like an Ass and Repeat Until You No Longer Look Like a Bumbling Idiot.

I have looked like an ass with a metal detector, coins, Texas hold em, photography, painting, knitting (never ever again), BBQ competitions, cooking, baking, and a whole list of other things the List of Ten got me into. Hey, learning is addicting (also another foreshadows of vol 2 but at this point I feel a little shame).

Back to the point. Get a book, read about the topic at hand, learn its rules. Everything has some. Go out into the world practicing those rules, being the bumbling idiot, we all are and then repeat. The books or learning material will make more sense this time around. Finally, you will have some real-world context. Go out into the world, practice and look like less of a bonehead and repeat. At some point you will be a master. Probably after 10,000 hours but only spend that amount of time if the topic is a true passion. Don't be afraid to give up and find some new things to apply this rule to. Knitting...not for me. Ever. Anything that involves plant life, also not for me. I like to be good to nature, not kill it. Sooner or later you will find a magical place that deserves 10,000 hours.

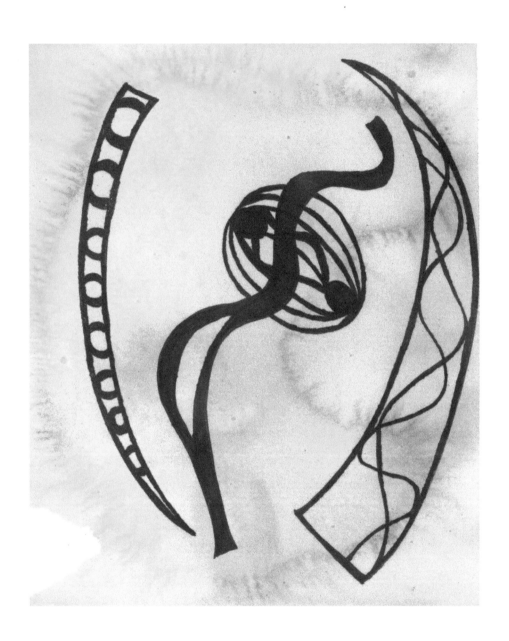

Sometimes A Do Over Is Necessary

I am not even going to tell you this rule. Rather I shall share a story about my art installation this book was to be based on. The stories about this installation could be a book on their own. Truth be told. those stories are fighting to get out. I chose to let this story win.

I had three completed pieces. Each had titles. Each were painted at the same time. This one battled me like the little demon spawn art pieces can and will be.

This piece was so demanding that when I took the border tape off, it tore some of the painting off. It was screaming at me that I had gotten it wrong! We fought! There I was in one corner and there the piece was in another corner (with no referee to bet on, I might add). That little tear of the painting was saying "No perfection. There must be a do over."

Here is the thing; A complete do over was not required. I had gotten the name wrong. The name needed a do over. All three of these pieces needed it. What can I say? I gave them each other's names. The name of the torn piece belonged to one that did not represent needing a do over, (or at least not like this one demanded). Thankfully I had a demanding piece that wasn't going to let me eat, sleep, breathe or eat the pizza waiting for me until the do over happened.

You see, that is the beauty of art behind the scenes. it proves its point just like my story and this piece prove the rule.

Always Have an Escape Plan A, B, And C

In the spirit of honesty; there are things we must do that we desperately do not want to do. We just want to escape. To set yourself up to succeed, I suggest multiple escape plans. You can break these escape plans into types so that all your bases are covered.

It might be that time is a good way to plot these plans, say a 30-minute leave plan, 45-minute leave plan and the ever awful 60 minutes of suffering plan. These types of plans work for short-term problems. If it is a long-term problem then you might want a 6-month, 1-year or even the dreaded two-years-of-endurance-plan.

The beauty of these types of plans is that one failure... with proper effort put in...ensures ever greater rates of success on plan B or C. The key is to execute all parts of the plan knowing that the greatest rate of success is plan C, but that earlier plans have potential. Of course, you must be always building towards plan C.

The golden rule of all the plans is that you show some damn discipline on each part of the plan. See it does not matter what the plans are if there is action. Every single action leads to a greater success rate. So, plot a course and do not get stuck on Gilligan's Island through inaction. Bam! Success. It is that simple.

Perspective, Everyone Has One

Don't be The Jerk. You have a right to your perspective but so does everyone else. No two are alike. Perspectives are created like snowflakes, unique and original as the life or conditions that made them. That is utterly amazing. Do not take that away from another living person, or you will be The Jerk.

Be vehement, be dedicated to, and protective of your perspective. Most of all, allow that for every other individual you encounter. All individuals are a result of conditions beyond their control just like a snowflake.

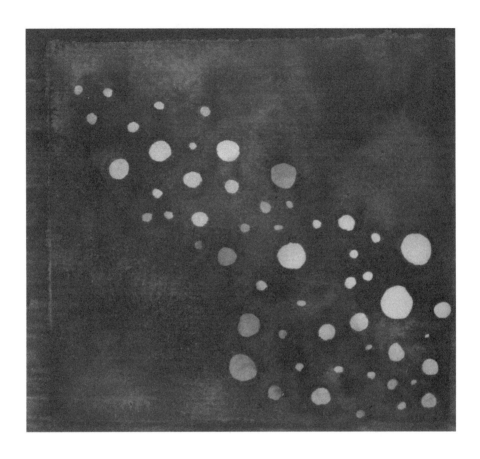

Everyone Needs A Rock No One Needs an Anchor

Funny story. This piece was going to be the anchor of the original version of my installation. It was going to sit near the bottom right of the installed work. Holding it there, anchoring everything.

Art might need an anchor point in the work, but people never do. Anchors do not ground you. They pull you down into the murky depths of algae infested...Oh wait that was a near death experience I had once. The point is true though. Anchors pull you down and pin you to finite space. While being secure might be good, not moving is bad too far from that spot.

A rock (not a rock that is so large that even God can't lift it) on the other hand comes along for the ride. A gentle reminder of all the things you hold dear and true.

Those people in your inner circle are either rocks or anchors. Me? I get rid of the anchors that cause near-death-as-in-my-life-flashed-before-my-eyes-incidents. So, should you.

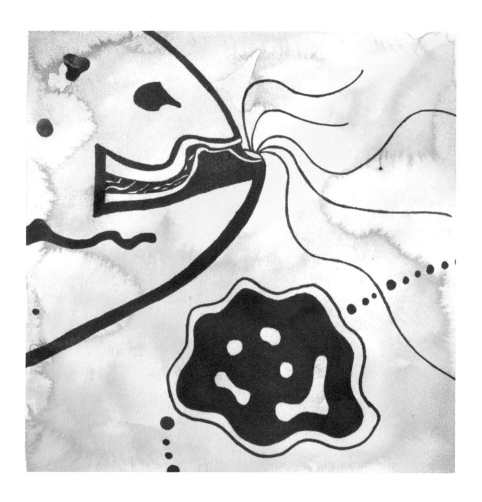

You Get One Day To Feel Sorry For Yourself

Oh, my. How cold and heartless I am. I get it. The world can toss a lot of decaying salamanders at you. They pile up and it gets tough to not feel sorry for yourself.

Pity - especially self-pity - is just a cover up for the real feelings you need to feel. Here is my example. I feel sorry for myself regarding a vision issue that was a result of being hit by a drunk driver. Pity quickly drains my energy. Pity eats energy like it is the last taco in the world. Things that zap your energy are never good.

Take your day. Lay on the couch with chip crumbs on you, not showering, lethargically lazing the day away. Wrap yourself up on the blanket of knowledge that today is the day you get to do this thing called a pity party.

The next day identify and live with the real emotions. I was angry. Very angry. Not that I got hit by a drunk driver but rather that the universe thought I needed yet another roadblock to plow through. What the hell, universe? Once I embraced that anger, I could see past it and look for ways to move to acceptance. When you are in the midst of a Pity Party...no way you are seeing acceptance because acceptance takes energy and hard work.

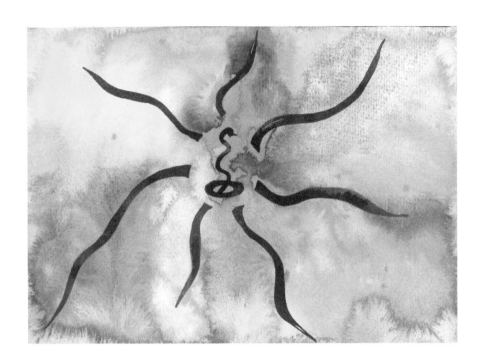

Do No Harm

This is the advice where you get to tell me I am not brilliant. "Do No Harm" is a horrid life motto to live by. It sounds easy, right? It sounds righteous. It is on top of my pile of rules I live by. It is the hardest rule to live by. This is the one that trips me up every time.

Let me tell you the truth. It is the most difficult of all the rules. Define harm, I dare you. Sure, not littering is not doing harm. Not lying is doing no harm. Following most sets of laws and rules is not doing harm. What about when it gets difficult?

White lies? Do they harm? Telling someone a painful truth? Not telling someone a painful truth? Wait....Do what I did and dig in to this never-ending pit of a question; 'what is harm'. The longer you do it the more you realize everyone has their own path. You can't define harm for anyone but you. In that defining you may take action that IS causing harm.

And what then? Littering seems somehow irrelevant. I mean for real, why is that not just a known - no one should litter? We give all this time effort and thought to the obvious. Do no harm is NOT obvious and requires constant contemplation at 4am or during the middle of that steak dinner, worse yet as you are conversing deeply with a friend. I hope you all believe me that THIS is the rule to consider NOT following as a life motto. On the other hand, it has its rewards.

Was this essay harmful? I like to think of it as reverse psychology, so I have all my bases covered.

Ball of Flames or Glorious Sunset All Endings In Grace

It is time for the "Don't be a train wreck' talk. I get it. It is hard to look away from a train wreck. I am not judging you, we have all been there watching the train wreck. Don't be the train wreck. I might not be able to look away. I will feel bad the entire time, but if you are a train wreck, that is the risk you run.

Endings happen. Every book, movie, song, relationship and life end. (I want to continue with second, minute, hour, day...Bad Idea yes?) Some endings are not as easy as others. Some truly are a ball of flames. Handle all of them with grace. This one piece of advice will save you years of self-recrimination. It is the life preserver when the ship sinks. This is the truth that stops you from hiding in the house for a year after the wreck. It is also the piece of advice that can lead you to the least amount of regret. It is the advice that makes moving forward easier.

Believe it or not, grace is important in good endings too. Sometimes an ending that is good for us is not good for others. Be graceful when that happens. Good sportsmanship does count. So, treat all endings as the beautiful sunset of one door opening while another closes. (I always wanted to mix those two metaphors together....cross one off the unofficial list of things to get done, that is not a foreshadowing of future Vols....I hope)

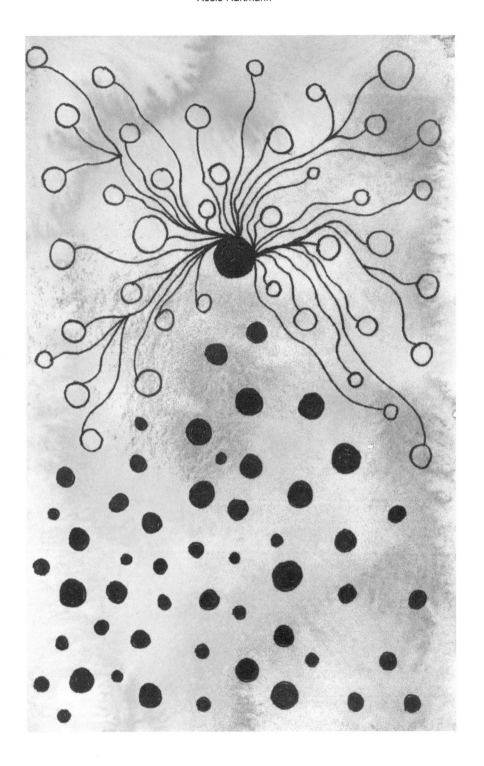

Feel the energy of every moment

This is the power advice. Come on you've said it; "I didn't see that coming". Maybe you could have. I am here to help you avoid stepping into a pile of hot steamy doggy doo doo or ruining a joyful moment for someone.

You walk into a room and you could cut the tension with a knife. You go outside and feel Spring coming. Every moment has energy that is changing at some undetermined pace. Sometimes you blink and it is different. Other times it has been the same for so long you consider it to be a rut. The only way you can know is to take a nanosecond (after practice, gaining awareness and whatever other caveat to ensure you don't think you can't do it) and notice it. Spring is easy - we all want to notice it. It is the routine moments we take for granted. Both require you to take a second or two to digest the energy of the moment.

Practice correctly and you can become a pro at knowing things before they happen. Being intuitive takes practice. Once you do that you can and should use your newly found super hero power for good. You can affect the energy with a well-placed joke, compliment or action. You've just got to feel the power of the energy in every moment to do it.

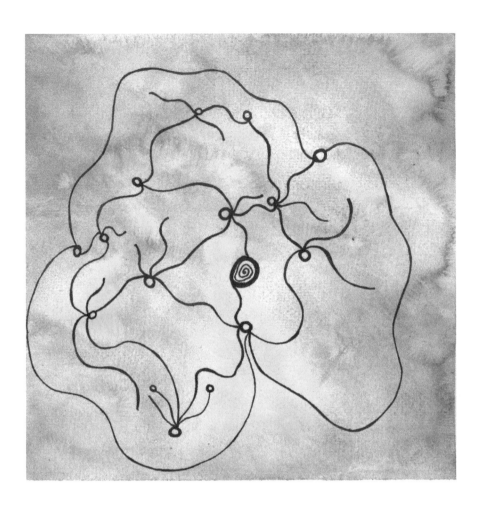

An Object in Motion Stays In Motion

If you want the secret to getting a ton done this is it. Once you sit down you may not get back up again. You can battle this by also working on things when you sit versus being a couch potato growing sprouts.

The weight of your body triples the minute you stop for a break that has no planned end time. Suddenly your feet are made of lead and your arms are titanium or kryptonite or some other type of material that seems to be draining the energy from your brain.

There is no rest for the wicked and there will be time to sleep at bed time. I would like to refer to the 80% Rule in all things. Which apparently wants to be included in Vol 2 but likely will not make an appearance ever. (I want you all to have an underdog you are rooting for while I let Little Monster dictate being a monster on this one, so that he thinks he has a win) Back on topic, 20% of the time it is okay to grow sprouts but that other 80% you've got to move it, move it!

Follow the Leader Is Only Fun Till Its Not

Trends, Gurus and master classes of perfection on every topic of today, (let's not forget fashion, music and movies), all lead to slow death of the soul.

If I followed the Gurus, I would have 5 websites, 5 of every social media and 5 separate but consistent voices. In what reality does that sound like fun?

I did not mind being told how to dress when I was five. Today - not fun. Also, I love superheroes but face it the market is a little saturated. Not to mention reboots. Where are the original ideas? Where/when does anyone care about MY time or sense of art and such?

Therefore, your personal vow is "Follow the Leaders" is only fun till it's not and then don't. Be you. Shine. Be different. Drop the stuff that sucks your soul dry. Sure, there might be a price to pay for it, but it is a choice. The world needs righteous, creative, wonderful, unique people and leaders. So, when following is no longer fun go do what is right for you.

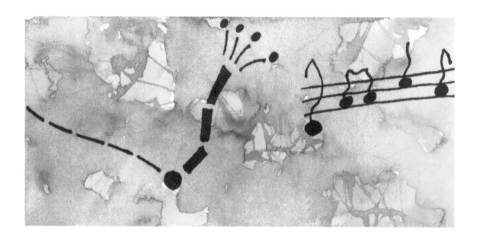

Pick a damn good song to live life to

There is a song for every season, turn, turn, turn....

I lost count a while back on all the song references that are packed into this rather tiny amount of writing. I hope they did not smack you in the face. If they did my defense is being bold. If I got one or more stuck in your head, I consider my job here done.

At the risk that no songs got stuck in your head...

Songs help us set a rhythm. Music gets your brain moving in a different way. Tunes make the physical body react in joy and sorrow. Honesty means admitting that sometimes we all need help in expressing ourselves. Music is a natural at this job. Have a song that represents your life. Mine: "Sticks and Stones" by Jonsi (From the greatest animated movie of all time, How to Train Your Dragon).

Every person that has meaning to me in my life has a song that represent them to me. If I need a little bit of My Pops today, I crank "Whiskey for My Horses". Every mood has a song or five to keep me going. If I want inspiration and motivation, I turn up the volume on Eminem. Anger much? Lincoln Park; "Burn it Down". The songs for all occasions list grows every time a song hits me in some magical way.

Sure, maybe I go too far for you with music. You do not need a song for everything, just a few things. They help. More importantly, what you listen to impacts how you are feel in that moment. So how do you want to feel? Play a song like that. On repeat. For four hours or four days. Whatever it takes.

Don't Cross the Line

How is that for vague advising? What line? I have no clue. All I know is this: I know it right as I walk up to it and tread too close to it. Every instinct in me is screaming. All the aspects of me are yelling. And then… there is a moment of hesitation.

What am I doing so close to this imaginary line? How did I get here? When did this place and time become a line? Well my friend let me tell you, consider each of these pieces of advice, within this book, as a possible line you could cross at any moment. After this book you will be asking yourself the same damn thing – how did I get close to this line?

Life if full of these dangerous lines. It is amazing I ever leave the house! Even that would be crossing a line though.

The trick is to define the lines so that you know when you are treading close to them. Once you know it, you have a choice; Run straight across it, Duck and Cover or carefully walk back from the line.

When you do this enough times, you realize even your lines have lines. I pray I do not discover one day that the lines that have lines have lines as well.

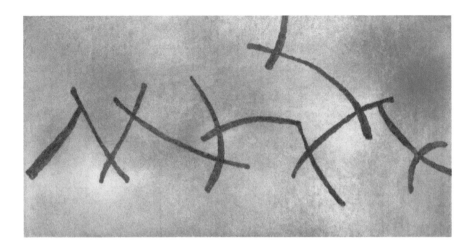

Liberate yourself break the rules

Joy is breaking rules. No, do not become a criminal. What I mean is this; once you learn the rules you can break them to perfection, thereby liberating yourself from the confines we humans like to create for everything. This act is called freedom.

Freedom. Think about that word for a minute. What does it mean to you? I get to create what I want, when I want and how I want. This includes my life and everything in it.

My Inner Child loves this advice. I hear her screaming "Yahoo!" in the background. Once you know the rules your inner kid gets to play. If you do not know what that feels like, go out today and get some finger paints (water soluble, only please). Sit at the kitchen table and finger paint on the wall. Go wild. Make a night or even a drinking game out of it. If this does not make your eyes sparkle in delight and glee let loose, have a shot and repeat. Loosen up some, your Inner Child needs some love and breaking the rules always does the trick.

This is also the "thing" that brings it all full circle. This is not a cliff-hanger ending. It is a revolving door. Go out, brave soul, Arise, Go Forth, Conquer the very scary world, not needing the win because revolving doors only go in a ciruclar motion.

You can follow this potential train wreck in the following ways:

Facebook: @StudioRosie
www.studiorosie.com
Ebay: rosiej

There will be experiments, celebrations, failures and inevitably some comic relief along the way. Be warned, I am an interactive participator.

CPSIA information can be obtained
at www.ICGtesting.com
Printed in the USA
BVHW021534300419
546961BV00014B/152/P